The Fosdyke Saga

Alan Plater

A Samuel French Acting Edition

SAMUELFRENCH-LONDON.CO.UK
SAMUELFRENCH.COM

Copyright © 1978 by Alan Plater and Bill Tidy
All Rights Reserved

THE FOSDYKE SAGA is fully protected under the copyright laws of the British Commonwealth, including Canada, the United States of America, and all other countries of the Copyright Union. All rights, including professional and amateur stage productions, recitation, lecturing, public reading, motion picture, radio broadcasting, television and the rights of translation into foreign languages are strictly reserved.

ISBN 978-0-573-11135-8

www.samuelfrench-london.co.uk

www.samuelfrench.com

FOR AMATEUR PRODUCTION ENQUIRIES

UNITED KINGDOM AND WORLD
EXCLUDING NORTH AMERICA
plays@SamuelFrench-London.co.uk
020 7255 4302/01

Each title is subject to availability from Samuel French,
depending upon country of performance.

CAUTION: Professional and amateur producers are hereby warned that *THE FOSDYKE SAGA* is subject to a licensing fee. Publication of this play does not imply availability for performance. Both amateurs and professionals considering a production are strongly advised to apply to the appropriate agent before starting rehearsals, advertising, or booking a theatre. A licensing fee must be paid whether the title is presented for charity or gain and whether or not admission is charged.

The professional rights in this play are controlled by Alexandra Cann Representation, 4 Montpelier Street London, SW7 1EE.

No one shall make any changes in this title for the purpose of production. No part of this book may be reproduced, stored in a retrieval system, or transmitted in any form, by any means, now known or yet to be invented, including mechanical, electronic, photocopying, recording, videotaping, or otherwise, without the prior written permission of the publisher. No one shall upload this title, or part of this title, to any social media websites.

The right of Alan Plater to be identified as author of this work has been asserted by him in accordance with Section 77 of the Copyright, Designs and Patents Act 1988

CHARACTERS

Actor 1
Actor 2
Actor 3 } as themselves
Actor 4
Actress 1
Actress 2

MAIN RUNNING CHARACTERS

Josiah Fosdyke
Rebecca Fosdyke
Tim Fosdyke
Victoria Fosdyke
Albert Fosdyke
Roger Ditchley

SUPPLEMENTARY CHARACTERS

Ben Ditchley
Mrs Pankhurst
Emily O'Malley
Pitman
Reporter
Warder
H.M. the King
M.C.
Officer
Schmidt
Baron von Richthoven
The Salford Ripper
Policeman
Newsboys

The action takes place in England mainly during the early part of the twentieth century

THE FOSDYKE SAGA

is based on the cartoon and characters
of "The Fosdyke Saga" appearing in the *Daily Mirror*.

MUSIC FOR THE PLAY

All enquiries regarding the music for the play
should be addressed to Samuel French Ltd.

ACT I

As the audience comes in, the performers—in costume but as themselves—chat up and generally make friends with the audience: selling signed photographs, conning drinks, discussing the day's football or racing—or anything else, according to time, place and the nature of the company

The show is performed in front of a simple, booth show type of backcloth, which bears a series of captions or visual images in the Bill Tidy style. This can be operated like a roller towel, or like a wallpaper display unit—whichever is easier. Captions and images are flexible. At the start of the show it reads THE FOSDYKE SAGA, though it could equally read SAFETY CURTAIN or SPONSORED BY KLEENEX—it is that kind of show. Props, musical instruments, funny hats, can lie around. When the concensus of opinion on stage is that no more people are likely to come in, the show starts with a little ad lib chat along the lines of "Are you ready?", "Shall we start?", "Check your flies", etc. The lines can be shared among the performers to taste: this is a head arrangement only. The song must be sung by the best ethnic-type folklorist in the gang—and so on

The lights go up on stage. The House lights go down. An ominous fanfare or drum roll sounds, and we are away

Actress 1 Good evening, ladies and gentlemen. Out of the melting pot of the industrial revolution came the class structure as we know it today. Tonight we will examine the opportunities available to the indigenous working classes for socio-econo-mobility within that class structure. Every word spoken here tonight is taken from contemporary source material—except the bits we made up ourselves. The time is nineteen hundred and two.
Actor 2 Nineteen hundred and three, isn't it?
Actress 1 The place—the Industrial North.
Actor 2 Lancashire.
Actor 4 Home of oppressed working-class sons and daughters of toil ...
Actor 1 Flogging their guts out in cotton mill and coalmine.
Actress 2 And in the manufacture of oppressed working class food.
Actress 1 Like cowheels, pigs' trotters, black pudding and tripe.
Actor 3 Ladies and gentlemen. A traditional ethnic folk song sung by the tripe workers of Lancashire in nineteen hundred and two ...
Actor 2 Nineteen hundred and three ...
Actor 3 Or nineteen hundred and three, when they were feeling oppressed, which I wrote myself as a project when a student at Birmingham Polytechnic Liberal Studies Department.

Actor 3 and the Company sing the song in an exaggerated "Oh-Come-Ye" style

(*Singing*)
>Oh come all ye tripe mechanics
>A song I'll sing to you
>Of how our wives and babies starved
>In nineteen hundred and two
>We starved in nineteen hundred and three
>And four and five as well
>In six and seven and eight and nine
>We starved like bloody hell.

Chorus But don't sing fol de rol de rie
>Derry down and d'ye ken John Peel
>Shove your hands into your pockets
>And get the ethnic feel.

Actor 3 Oh L. S. Lowry he was there
>James Joyce was on the beer
>George Orwell he was in his pram
>Paying homage to Wigan Pier
>Old D. H. Lawrence he stood by
>All radical and sad
>Dodging the bricks and bottles thrown
>By Adrian Mitchell's Dad.

During the applause, the screen changes to read GRIDDLESBURY 1902 OR 1903, and bears a Tidyesque drawing of a pit-head

Actor 2 Industrial Lancashire. I'd know it anywhere.

During the following sequence, the company carry out minimal costume changes necessary to assume Fosdyke characters. Dialogue can be switched around to suit the mechanics of the operation

Actor 1 Griddlesbury, Lancashire, nineteen hundred and two, or nineteen hundred and three.

Actor 4 Population, five thousand and six . . .

A baby's cry is heard

>Five thousand and seven.

Actress 1 All oppressed as hell.
Actor 3 Sharing one dank earth closet.
Actress 2 Twenty-nine pawnshops.
Actor 2 Four hundred and sixty-nine pubs.
Actress 1 An age of Edwardian elegance.
Actor 3 And Dickensian squalor.
Actor 4 The Empire was in the ascendant.
Actress 2 But mostly people went to the Hippodrome.
Actor 2 Where topping the bill was T. S. Eliot, the famous Chocolate Coloured Coon.
Actor 1 But in Griddlesbury, Lancashire, there was no elegance, no fancy clothes, and precious little food and shelter for the Fosdyke Family.

The Fosdykes are now assembled, all in a line, and all in character

Act I

Josiah There was no champagne and oysters for Josiah Fosdyke. (*He gives a slight bow to the audience*)
Becky No crinolines or fol-de-rols for Rebecca Fosdyke. (*She curtsies*)
Tom No playing-fields of Eton for young Tom Fosdyke. (*He bows*)
Vicky No ladies-in-waiting for Victoria Fosdyke. (*She curtsies*)
Albert No ladies-in-waiting for little Albert Fosdyke. (*He bows*)
Becky Just poverty and degradation.
Josiah And a bloody big queue for the earth closet.

Josiah hammers on an imaginary door. We hear the banging

(*Shouting*) Who's in there? Huddersfield Choral Union?

The ringing of the pithead bell is heard

Can't you hear the pit bell? I should be at work.
Becky You'll just have to cross your legs and go, Josiah.
Vicky Don't go down the mine, Daddy.

Josiah puts on a pit helmet. Albert and Tom have a pee against the screen, watched by Vicky

Josiah I've got to, petal. So as to feed you and your mother and young Tom. Stop it, Victoria, you'll go blind—and little Albert.
Becky (*to the audience*) He's a good husband and father. A fine man.
Josiah Aye—I gave little Albert a bag of marbles only yesterday.
Albert But I'd eaten them by dinner-time.

The bell rings again

Josiah The pit is calling me to the bosom of The Good Earth.
Becky He's always known a good bosom when he sees one.

Josiah goes down the pit. He stands up straight then slowly bends down and mimes going down in the cage

Tom (*singing*) Close the coalhouse door, lads, There's blood inside.

Darkness. The pit caves in; there is a loud explosion. The Lights come up

A Pitman rushes on—played by the Ditchley actor

Pitman There's been a massive cave-in down Number Three shaft. They're bringing them up now.

Coughing noises are heard off, then Josiah crawls in, blackened and bruised

The Pitman meets him, concealing a banner on a pole

Becky Was Josiah t'only man trapped?
Pitman Aye, he was that. (*To Josiah*) Can you walk, old lad?
Josiah Aye—just about.
Pitman Well get walking, blackleg! (*He reveals a banner that reads: STRIKE NOW FOR 2d. A WEEK*)

The remainder of the company become Strikers by donning cloth caps and picking up banners, etc.

Chorus Scum, scab, blackleg, out out out! Scum, scab, blackleg, out out out! (*They stop sharply on an invisible cue*)
Josiah (*out of the silence*) I had to work through the strike, Rebecca. To buy little luxuries like bread and dripping.
Becky Nobody's speaking to us, Jos. They've smashed both the windows at the hovel.
Tom They've banned us from using the earth closet.
Becky Let's go away. I don't want Tom and Victoria and Albert and Tim to have the sort of life we've had ...
Josiah Tim! That's a new one on me.
Becky It was the shock of the accident brought him on.

Simultaneous with the above line a Baby is thrown to Becky by our spare actor, rugby league style

Josiah That settles it!

Josiah takes Baby Tim from Becky, none too gently

Josiah I'm taking you away from the squalor and degradation. I shall lead the Fosdyke Family into the Promised Land.
Tom The Promised Land?
Albert You mean America?
Josiah I mean Manchester.

Fanfare

Tom Where the streets are studded with meat pies.
Josiah Climb aboard, my family.

The Company simultaneously set up and climb into the "Train"—a simple cut-out carriage—strictly two-dimensional and marked PIG CLASS. There might be a couple of wheels that go round. A blast is blown on a whistle. The spare actor moves the screen on to give a fairly clumsy effect of movement— what happens in reality is that we move from the grimy Griddlesbury landscape to an identical landscape titled MANCHESTER. The journey might be supplemented by some clanking train noises and in any case there is some smoke. Against all this, the following dialogue continues

Becky They say that people in Manchester cough different, is that right, Josiah?
Josiah Aye, things are better there. Get on wi' your pig's trotter, Albert.
Vicky It looks very pretty, the scenery.
Josiah It's right pastoral, is Manchester.

The screen stops. There is a blast on a whistle and anybody who is available shouts

Anybody Manchester!
Tom That was quick.
Josiah Manchester welcomes the Fosdyke Family.

They alight from the train. Josiah reacts. He has seen Ben Ditchley standing on the station platform—our spare actor, now dressed in top hat and frock-coat—a gentleman, no less

Act I

You see that! That's a gentleman. Manchester's full of them.
Tom What are they for, Father?
Josiah You bow, you curtsey, you grovel—like this.
All Boss, squire, sir, your grace, your lord, your majesty. (*Accompanied by an obsequious grovelling routine of bowing, scraping, forelock-touching and such*)
Ditchley I think I'd better introduce myself. Ben Ditchley's the name.
All Not Ben Ditchley, t'Lancashire Tripe King?
Ditchley Aye. Ben Ditchley, t'Lancashire Tripe King.
Josiah Becky, you'll never guess who this is. It's Ben Ditchley, t'Lancashire Tripe King.
Ditchley Your child appears to have been covered in soot as a result of the journey ...

Ditchley wipes the baby's face with a piece of tripe from his top pocket

Josiah Oh, don't worry about it, sir, he's all right.
Ditchley No, no, do allow me.

And lo! the face is clear—result of using a prop doll with a swivel-head and two faces, one clean, one dirty. Gasps of awe!

Becky Young Tim's face restored to virgin whiteness by Ditchley's famous tripe.
Ditchley Do keep it with my compliments.
All Oh, thank you, Mr Ditchley.
Ditchley Now do I infer that you have come to Manchester in search of gainful employment of an honest nature?
Josiah I hope to improve my circumstances, sir.
Ditchley Fosdyke, will you work for me? Two shillings a week and all t'tripe you can eat?
Josiah It's a deal, Mr Ditchley, you'll not regret the day.
Ditchley (*to the audience*) One searching look was enough for me. You can always trust a man who tucks his shirt *inside* his underpants. (*He turns to Josiah*) Now then, Fosdyke, have you got somewhere to stay tonight?
Josiah Oh we'll find a nice warm bridge to sleep under, sir.
Ditchley Good. In that case, report to my factory at three o'clock in t'morning.
Becky Three o'clock in t'morning?
Ditchley Aye. Seeing as it's his first day—and we'll set you on in the Scalding Room—make a job of that, we'll happen promote you to slitting ...
All Thank you, Mr Ditchley.
Ditchley I'll give you fair warning, Fosdyke. What I like to see in my men is honesty and sobriety. Look not upon the wine when it is red.
Josiah Mr Ditchley. You're speaking to a past membership secretary of the Griddlesbury and District Sons of Temperance.
Ditchley A temperance man?
Becky He never goes anywhere without his banjo.

The following dialogue is adjusted to suit musical abilities of the company, as they assemble their instruments

Josiah She never goes anywhere without her spoons.
Tom And she never goes anywhere without her tambourine.
Vicky And he never goes anywhere without his big drum.
Albert And he never goes anywhere without his triangle.
Ditchley And I happen to have my guitar with me.
Josiah Hallelujah, brothers and sisters.
All Hallelujah.

They are lined up, instruments at the ready, for the song: an old-fashioned, Sally Army rousing hymn

Josiah Water Bright is my delight
I drink only what I ought to
Truly I glimpse Heaven's Gates
When I am passing water.

All When he is passing
He is passing
He is passing water
When he is passing
He is passing
He is passing water.

Josiah Piles of money bring no joy
Rich men live in misery
I can cure their misery
I can cure their piles.

All He can cure them
He can cure them
He can cure their piles
He can cure them
He can cure them
He can cure their piles.

Josiah Mortal sin sat on my brow
Water Bright has washed it off
Mortal sin has left me now
I have had it off.

All I have had it
I have had it
I have had it off
I have had it
I have had it
I have had it off.
Amen.

They add a few ad lib "Hallelujahs", etc. Then there is a reasonably holy silence, as Ditchley goes to Josiah

Act I

Ditchley Now, Fosdyke.
Josiah Aye.
Ditchley A resonant voice like that would be wasted in the Scalding Room. A soul that sings so purely must not prostitute its sweetness in the Slitting Shed.
Tom I think he's going to bestow a blessing.
Ditchley You shall have ...
Albert He *is* going to bestow a blessing.
Ditchley Your own tripe tray!
All His own tripe tray!
Ditchley Prepare thyself for t'ceremony.

They all hum a suitably noble theme—"Land of Hope and Glory" or "The Dambusters' March"—as Ditchley performs the ceremony of the laying-on of the tripe. Albert acts as a BBC commentator

Albert Josiah Fosdyke steps forward, right knee revealed, as he prepares to accept one of the highest accolades of the Manchester Tripe Fraternity. Mystic, poetic, ethnic, handed down with sticky fingers from generation to generation ...

Josiah kneels

Ditchley East is East.
All East is East.
Ditchley West is West.
All West is West.

Needless to say, the audience is cued to join in

Ditchley Ditchley's Tripe.
All Ditchley's Tripe.
Ditchley Is t'Best.
All Is t'Best.

Ditchley presents Josiah with a tray of tripe

Josiah Thank you, Mr Ditchley, that's very kind of you.
Ditchley Now. Go forth into the world with your tray.

Cheers from everybody. Josiah moves into the audience with his tripe tray. Dialogue can be adjusted to suit the people he meets and their reactions

    All except Becky exit

Becky works at her diary

Josiah Now who'd like their own personal piece of tripe? That they can handle all by themselves. You can get to know tripe really intimately this evening. There you are, dear, when you've felt it, perhaps you'd like to pass it round, let everybody have a feel. And you can have a bit over there as well. (*He throws a few pieces ad lib around the house*). And you can eat it as well. It's lovely with salt, and vinegar or you can have it straight. There you are, love, get to know it, it could be the start of a beautiful relationship. All right, Becky?

Becky is ready with her diary. As she speaks Josiah leaves the audience and disappears behind the screen

Becky Rebecca Fosdyke's diary. May or June nineteen-oh-six or nineteen-oh-seven. Josiah is progressing most encouragingly with his tripe round in the better areas of Manchester.

Josiah All sorts of tripe. Nuform, Fetherlite, Black Shadow, Gossamer, under plain wrapper.

Becky He spends all day practising his street cries of Old Moss Side. I might have to stop him. Today being Tuesday or Wednesday, I composed my usual sonnet and decided it should celebrate my feelings for Manchester, our new home. Sonnet by Rebecca Fosdyke, aged forty-six —or forty-seven.

> Leeds hath not anything to show more fair
> Thick as short planks be he who would pass by
> A cloud so noxious in intensity
> Manchester now doth like a string vest wear
> The dankness of the morning: surly folk,
> Pubs, pawnshops, doggy dirt and knackers' yards
> And drunken Irish navvies playing cards
> All dull and spluttering in the acrid smoke
> Never did muck more masochistic crown
> In choking splendour, never to wash off.
> Never saw I a town so dirty brown
> Canal so sluggish like a smoker's cough.
> Dear God, the very houses seem to frown
> And all that mighty heart says: bugger off.

In addition to my joy and delight in this city which has become our new home, it is also most gratifying to see how well little Victoria is getting on with Mr Ditchley . . .

Victoria and Ditchley enter from either side and meet C

Ditchley Ah, little Victoria, what pretty beads, my dear.
Vicky Thank you, Mr Ditchley.
Ditchley Let me give you a personal conducted tour of the Scalding Room.
Vicky Thank you, Mr Ditchley.

Ditchley and Vicky disappear behind the screen. We hear a single feminine squeal: part surprise, but a hint of delight

Becky Only this morning he gave her a conducted tour of the Scalding Room.

Ditchley and Vicky emerge

Vicky Thank you, Mr Ditchley.

Act I

Ditchley Tomorrow, I shall show you the Scalding Room again.
Vicky Thank you, Mr Ditchley.

Ditchley exits—(again, according to our *conventions, not French's Editions)*

Becky It is also most gratifying to see how well little Victoria is getting on with Mr Ditchley's son and heir, Roger—the family resemblance is remarkable.

Roger "enters", possibly played by the same actor as plays his father?

Roger Ah, little Victoria—what a pretty frock . . .
Vicky Thank you, Mr Ditchley—Junior . . .
Roger Roger.
Vicky Thank you.
Roger Let me give you a conducted tour of the Slitting Shed.

Before she has time to answer, he whisks her round the back of the screen

Becky Only this afternoon he gave her a conducted tour—

Vicky squeals behind the screen, permits herself a slight double-take, then continues

—of the Slitting Shed.

Roger and Vicky emerge from behind the screen

Roger You must have found that fascinating.
Vicky (*breathlessly*) Thank you, Roger.
Roger In that case—let me show you—the Experimental Wing!
Vicky (*wearily*) Thank you, Roger.

As Roger drags Vicky behind the screen again (and exit), Josiah resumes his tripe sales in the audience

Josiah Now, who didn't get their own personal piece of tripe last time? Just try this against your cheek, my dear, I bet that's an experience you've not had before . . . Look at that! She hasn't gone red or anything. Perhaps she *has* had the experience before . . .

Ditchley enters

Ditchley Ah, Fosdyke! I'm right pleased with you, Fosdyke.

Josiah meets Ditchley, c

Josiah Thank you, Mr Ditchley. I've been selling them a "Recipe of the Day" round Salford. Look at this. Monday—Tripe in the Hole. Tuesday—Tripe in a Basket. Wednesday—Tripe Truffles. Thursday—Indian speciality, Tandoori Tripe. Friday—Chinese speciality—Tripe Foo Yung. Saturday—Tripe Mayonnaise. And on Sunday for tea—Tripe Trifle. (*He hands Ditchley the recipe list*)
Ditchley Very fascinating. (*He throws it away*) Thank you. Now listen,

Fosdyke. There's something else I want to talk to you about. That daughter of yours ...

Vicky squeals behind the screen, plus assorted scuffles and giggles

Josiah Little Victoria?
Ditchley She's built like a drayhorse. Mrs Ditchley's been dead these past ten years and to be quite frank I'm getting to be a bit cold in winter, if you follow my meaning.
Josiah Well we're very grateful for your kind interest, Mr Ditchley, but it's really up to Victoria herself.
Ditchley Joss. May I call you Joss?
Josiah Of course, Ben.
Ditchley Mr Ditchley.
Josiah Mr Ditchley.
Ditchley If you become my father-in-law there's a seat for you on West Lancashire Tripe Foundation Board.

Becky enters with a scream

Josiah An end to poverty, woman, and all you can do is scream.
Becky It's Victoria and young Roger. They've run away together!
Josiah Run away? Where to?
Becky I think they said Wigan.
Ditchley Wigan!
Josiah Good God! A suicide pact!

Ditchley clutches his heart and collapses in a heap

Quick, Becky, he's had a coronarary—a coronarary—a heart attack.

They manoeuvre Ditchley on to a bed or a convenient chair. Ditchley speaks quietly, sickly

Ditchley That no good wastrel son of mine, stealin' the lass I were going to wed ...
Becky There, there, don't take on so ...
Ditchley If I know bloody Roger, he'll have put her up the stick, the rotten, worthless waster, the ...
Josiah I'm sure you're mistaken, Mr Ditchley.

Ditchley straightens up angrily

Ditchley Are you saying my lad's not capable? (*He flops back, more or less unconscious*)
Becky (*to the audience*) Meanwhile, in Wigan ...

Vicky and Roger enter in bed. They stand in front of the screen, covered by a sheet so that it's a vertical bed and they play the scene standing up

Josiah—or anybody else convenient and available—sings a schmaltzy intro. to the scene

Act I

Josiah (*singing*) Once on a high and windy hill
   In the morning mist two lovers kissed
   And the world stood still . . .
Vicky Oh Roger, do you think your father will find us?
Roger Shut your gob, woman, I'm thinking.
Vicky Darling, let's get married and then they can never part us.
Roger Married?
Vicky Yes.
Roger You—a mere working-class strumpet, and me, a gentleman of breeding?
Vicky But what will happen to me?
Roger Have you ever heard of—Consolidated White Slavers of Birkenhead?

Vicky weeps

   Don't start all that. It moistens the atmosphere and makes my cigar wilt.
Vicky I sense you've grown cold towards me.
Roger I'm tired of you. You bore me.
Vicky But darling—I'm pregnant.

Ditchley opens one eye

   What have you got to say to that?

Pause

Roger Good-bye. (*He moves away from the bed, and puts on a top hat*)
Vicky You can't leave me like this.
Roger That's true. I'm forgetting my trousers and frock coat.

Roger grabs a pair of trousers and a frock coat and goes

Vicky gathers the sheet around herself. The music plays softly and sadly—"Department of Hearts and Flowers". We lose sight of everybody else on the stage, except for the recumbent Ditchley

Vicky A Maiden's Lament. (*She sings the song*)
   I'm a disenchanted maiden
   Whom a rotter did besmirch
   I am left with child a-pending
   Without benefit of church
   Oh the villain's name was Roger
   I believed he was a gent
   But the evidence a-growing
   Shows that he was pleasure bent.

We see signs of developing pregnancy under the sheet

   Oh he wooed and he cooed me
   Said my cheeks were in full bloom
   Said he'd teach me Ancient Wisdom

> In a Wigan small back room
> Oh he taught me and he taught me
> Taught me thrice without remorse
> If you're seeking Ancient Wisdom
> Take a correspondence course.

There is a short musical bridge while the picture on the screen is changed—either by Vicky herself or by one of the other actors. The picture, when it arrives, is of a bridge over a canal

During the course of the last verse, Vicky climbs steps behind the screen so that at the end she is, in effect, standing on the bridge

> Love is tender, love is thrilling
> Love is sweet but here's the rub
> You soon find that you are paying
> Your subscription to the club
> It's a story so familiar
> It's a story so banal
> That the proper place to end it
> Is the Salford Ship Canal.

She stands poised, ready to jump

> *At that moment, another woman climbs up beside her. It is Mrs Pankhurst, no less*

Mrs Pankhurst What are you doing, child?
Vicky I'm going to jump in the canal on account of I'm besmirched.
Mrs Pankhurst Allow me to introduce myself. Mrs Emmeline Pankhurst. I am going to jump into the canal on behalf of the Women's Suffrage Movement. In protest.
Vicky What are you protesting about?
Mrs Pankhurst The exploitation of Women by Men! (*She leaps into the audience and hits all adjacent men with a rolled-up copy of a radical newspaper*)

> *A surly Reporter enters*

(*Calling to Vicky*) The World's Press is here. All of him. I'm afraid you must allow me to jump first.
Vicky If I join your movement, we could jump together.
Mrs Pankhurst Very good. I'll bring up the enrolment forms.

Vicky signs the form

That'll be half-a-crown.
Vicky I'm sorry. I have no money. I'm a penniless working-class strumpet.

The Reporter shouts at them from the edge of the proceedings

Reporter Get on with it! Soon as this job's done we've all got to piss off to Sarajevo.
Mrs Pankhurst Very well, young lady. You can be our token working-

Act I

class strumpet. You can work off the half crown in protest jumps. Are you ready, gentlepigs—I mean men?
Reporter Bloody sexist.
Mrs Pankhurst One, two, three—jump!

Black-out. Two cries are heard; two big splashes, bubbling and gurgling. The Lights fade up gently on Ditchley's Death Scene. Ditchley is lying there, in the last peaceful moments; Josiah kneeling at the bedside

Ditchley I'm sinking fast, lad.
Josiah Aye, you're not the only one, Mr Ditchley.
Ditchley Tripeworks is yours, Jos.
Josiah Mine, Mr Ditchley, mine?
Ditchley You've been loyal and selfless in your devotion.
Josiah Mine!!
Ditchley And I've cut young Roger out of my will after what he did to me.
Josiah Mine!!!
Ditchley So it's all yours, lad. Well? What have you to say for yourself?
Josiah Could I have it in writing? Just a modest written agreement I took the liberty of drawing up in case of emergency, Mr Ditchley—just sign on the dotted line.

Josiah guides Ditchley's hand as they jointly sign a large document

Ben—jam—in . . .

Ditchley dies hereabouts

Ditchley!

Becky enters to see Josiah donning a top hat, taken from Ditchley's head

Becky Josiah—is he dead?
Josiah He'd better be. Look at that.

Becky reads the document

Becky You're—Master of Ditchley's?
Josiah Read it again. I'm Master of Fosdyke's. Let's see, I'll have a couple of them horseless carriages, a dozen grovelling servants, a billiard table and a balloon . . .
Becky Do you think I could have a new apron?
Josiah Now now, Rebecca, you mustn't let our new-found wealth go to your head . . .
Becky Oooh. I sense a change in you, Josiah, since you became Master of Ditchley's.
Josiah Fosdyke's!

The Reporter lets off a bright sparkler or flashbulb

What the bloody hell's that?
Reporter It's a newsflash, Mr Fosdyke.
Josiah Mr Fosdyke. By God, I like being called Mister. Get on with it, peasant.

On the screen a Sales Graph appears, going up and up

Reporter The Royal Tripe Exchange, Manchester, is buzzing with excitement at the rapid growth of the Fosdyke Tripe Empire.

Tom and Albert enter and stand either side of Josiah

Josiah Tom, Albert—we're smashing our competitors to smithereens with go-ahead sales techniques.
Tom But isn't that a little unkind, Father?
Josiah Don't be so namby-pamby, you great nance.
Albert Bad news, Father. General Booth, beloved leader of the Salvation Army, passed away today.
Josiah Bloody great.
Tom You seem pleased about it, Father.
Josiah Of course, you great girl's blouse! What do you think this is? (*He produces a piece of black, floppy substance from his pocket, and hands it to Tom*)
Josiah Black tripe! Every time a great public figure pegs out, we'll have mourning tripe on the streets within the hour.
Albert That's marvellous, Father.
Josiah And if it's royalty we'll get it embossed with little crowns all round the edges.
Reporter It is rumoured in the Tripe Exchange that Fosdykes are experimenting with a whole new range of special additives.
Tom Would you like to try this, Father? (*He hands Josiah a jar*)
Josiah What is it?
Albert That nice young doctor in the research laboratory sent it up for tasting.
Josiah (*tasting and gasping*) What the bloody hell is it?
Tom Pigs' ears in brine.
Josiah (*spitting it out*) Sack the feller immediately. What's his name?
Tom Crippen.
Josiah Bloody southerners. Get rid of him.
Reporter But an even more threatening shadow casts itself over the newly found Fosdyke prosperity ...
Josiah Shadows? What's he on about?
Albert Shall I ask him?
Josiah Aye, ask him.
Albert Shadows? What you on about?
Reporter Manchester, nineteen twelve or thirteen.
Josiah Stuff all that, tell us about the shadow.
Reporter Little Victoria Fosdyke languishes in Strangeways Prison, on hunger strike, all in support of the Suffragette cause ...
Tom Hunger strike?
Josiah Poor lass must be starving. I must visit my poor besmirched daughter.

Josiah goes to the prison door—imaginary of course. Tom and Albert

Act I

retreat. The Reporter puts on a prison officer's hat and picks up a bunch of keys

I'd like to see Victoria Fosdyke please, my man.
Warder Walk this way, sir.

Josiah follows the Warder, imitating his bizarre walk—whatever it is—round behind the screen and out again the other side. This can include the locking and unlocking of imaginary doors to taste

Hold on there, sir, and I'll go and fetch her.
Josiah Thank you.

The Warder exits

Josiah mimes treadmill bashing—perhaps with sound effects on

The Warder returns with Vicky

Vicky Father! What are you in for?
Josiah To see you, luv.
Warder Get moving, both of you.

Vicky gets on the treadmill and they play the scene on the move, with suitable music: e.g. "The Volga Boatman"

Josiah Come home, Victoria.
Vicky I can't, Father. I have devoted my life to the Suffrage Movement—they helped me in my hour of need. I have a child fathered by Roger Ditchley...
Josiah The filthy swine had his way with you and left? The scoundrel! Using my child and slinging his hook...
Vicky My comrades in the Movement have been so kind to me and the baby...
Josiah But we're in improved circumstances now—we can bring up your son so that one day he can take his proper place in the business...
Vicky It's a girl, Father.

Josiah stops suddenly, aghast

Josiah A girl! A rotten lousy snivelling girl! I was hoping for a boy. Anyone can knock a hole in an old tin can but it takes a man to put a spout on it.
Vicky Besides, I cannot betray the Movement. I am about to make the supreme sacrifice.
Josiah The canal again, is it?
Vicky On Saturday it's the Derby. I'm going to throw myself under the King's horse.
Josiah You can't do that!
Vicky It's my bounden duty.
Josiah But I've got a fiver each way on the King's horse.
Vicky Show my Father out, Warder.

The Warder picks up Josiah and flings him out in another heap

Josiah *Show* me out, she said.
Warder Sorry, sir, force of habit—know what I mean?

Josiah moves to where Becky, Tom and Albert are waiting

Josiah Very bad news, love. She's made up her mind to throw herself under the King's horse.
Becky Oh Jos. What are we going to do?
Josiah All we can do is pray.

They kneel in prayer

Tom Are we praying for Victoria?
Josiah You three pray for Victoria. I'll pray for the horse.

Pause. Then a voice is heard off

Voice (*off*) Paper, paper, read all about it!

A newspaper is thrown over the screen. Albert picks it up and reads—great drama!

Albert Big headlines ...
All Big headlines ...
Albert Suffragette throws herself ...
All Suffragette throws herself ...
Albert Under the King!
All Under the King?
Albert Vicky's alive and His Majesty was only shaken.
Josiah Our prayers were answered. I must send five shillings to the Methodists.
Becky But the shame of it! The anger of the Nation!

There is a loud hammering at the door

Tom That must be the Nation at the door now.
Josiah Don't be afraid, Tom.

Another loud hammering

You answer it—go on, you big girl's blouse!

Tom goes to answer the door

Tom returns, grovelling, followed by H.M. the King. We might well use a slab of regal music over this entry—a touch of the Elgars, maybe

Josiah Can you ever forgive us, your—your ...
Albert Try Majesty.
Josiah Your Majesty ...
Becky Show us the way to the Tower—but give us time to change our underwear—er, personal clothing ...

The King—George V to be precise—allows a decent regal pause

King I could have been severely injured, it is true. Happily, your daughter struck me with her—er—blunt end.

Act I

Josiah Even so, I trust the experience did not cause you undue distress—your . . .
Becky Majesty . . .
Josiah I know, you stupid cow.
King On the contrary. It was a most enjoyable experience. Kneel, Fosdyke.

The King brings his sword from its scabbard and places it on Josiah's shoulder

Josiah No, it's Josiah Fosdyke actually, sir.
King Arise, Sir Josiah Fosdyke.
Josiah Sir Josiah?
All Sir Josiah?
Josiah I'll send seven-and-six to the Methodists.

Vicky enters, smiling at the King

King Ah, Victoria—thank you once more for showing me the—er—Slitting Shed. So interesting meeting my subjects from North of Watford. 'Bye 'bye.

The King makes a regal exit, with a final flash of regal music

Josiah Fosdykes, arise!
Becky You what?
Vicky Is it the National Anthem?
Josiah No, it is not. It's the Fosdyke Anthem.

Josiah waves an imperious arm, which produces a drum roll, and out of that, the song

Chorus Fosdykes Arise
Fosdykes Arise
Lift up thine eyes
See the Fosdykes Arise.

Josiah I will disdain
Sardines and kippers
I'll drink champagne
From ladies' slippers
I will drink wine
I shall get plastered
I'll be a swine
I'll be a bastard.

Chorus Fosdykes Arise
Fosdykes Arise
Lift up thine eyes
See the Fosdykes Arise.

Becky I shall acquire
Ladylike status
Eat caviare
No more potaters

I'll quash the mean
Ill-founded rumours
Never be seen
Without my best bloomers.

Chorus Fosdykes Arise
Fosdykes Arise
Lift up thine eyes
See the Fosdykes Arise.

Tom I shall be good
Unspoiled by riches
Eat simple food
Dig lots of ditches
Stick to my roots
And love my neighbour
Wear shiny boots
And even Vote Labour.

Josiah (*speaking*) I'm worried about him.

Chorus Fosdykes Arise
Fosdykes Arise
Lift up thine eyes
See the Fosdykes Arise.

Becky Come on, Victoria, sock it to them, darling.

Vicky There in the sky
See my vocation
Searching for my
Emancipation
When I assume
My true position
I will resume
Normal transmission.

Chorus Fosdykes Arise
Fosdykes Arise
Lift up thine eyes
See the Fosdykes Arise.

Albert I shall command
Men of all station
I shall demand
Due adoration
I shall expect
Touching of forelocks
Or they'll collect
A kick in the borelocks.

Chorus (*a big and noble finish*)
Fosdykes Arise

Act I

>   Fosdykes Arise
>   Lift up thine eyes
>   See the Fosdykes Arise.

Josiah I'm not worried about him though. (*He pats Albert on the shoulder*)
Becky Isn't it wonderful? We're all so happy.

Roger Ditchley pops his head over the top of the screen

Roger Your happiness is built on shifting sands.
All What? Pardon? (*etc.*)
Becky I didn't say anything.
Josiah Something about sand.
Roger The drums of war are beating.
Albert Something about drums.
Josiah Oh never mind about that. Let's all get back to work. Now how's business, Albert?

All exit except Josiah and Albert. Roger bobs down behind the screen

Albert Fan-bloody-tastic Father. All our drivers are meeting their quotas.

On the screen a map of Manchester appears

Josiah Aye, you can't beat a good incentive scheme for making the fellers work.
Albert What is the incentive scheme this week?
Josiah Wages.

A pigeon flies over the screen and lands on the stage

Josiah What the bloody hell's that?
Albert Second post.
Josiah Is it dead?
Albert No, just stage-struck. (*He picks up the pigeon and reads the message*) There's been an unexplained ninety-four per cent drop in sales in Gas Street.
Josiah You'd best investigate it, son. Off you go.

Albert exits and crosses with a breathless and urgent Tom

Tom There's trouble in Canal Street, Dad.
Josiah What sort of trouble?
Tom One of our drivers attacked and stuffed with cowheels.
Josiah There's summat nasty brewing, I can feel it in my water.

Roger pops his head over the top of the screen

Roger Shifting sands. I did warn them.
Josiah Why do you keep on about sand?
Tom I didn't say anything.
Josiah (*looking at the map*) You'd best check there's nothing going on in Didsbury, that's a dead rough area.
Tom Right.

Tom exits, crossing with Albert, who is carrying something behind his back

Albert There's been another evil incident, Father.

Another explosion on the screen

Josiah Tell us the worst.

Albert The Sandringham Tenements for the Aged and the Incontinent. One of our drivers. Victim of a savage pickled onion attack. He's in hospital.

Josiah A pickled onion put him in hospital?

Albert It was in a four-pound jar. (*He produces the jar*)

Josiah You'd best get down and investigate it, son—quick as you can.

Albert Right.

Albert exits, crossing with a very serious-faced Tom

Tom It's getting worse, Father.

Josiah Aye, what now?

Tom In Didsbury. One of our drivers. The ultimate sanction.

Pause

Josiah The ultimate sanction?

Tom Yes . . .

Josiah Not . . . ?

Tom Yes . . .

Josiah But . . .

Tom I know . . .

Josiah That hasn't happened since Burnley in eighteen ninety-six . . .

Tom I'm sorry, Father. He's been—tarred and triped.

Josiah Tarred and triped. There hasn't been a tarring and triping since . . .

Tom / **Josiah** Burnley in eighteen ninety-six (*speaking together*)

Albert enters

Albert Good news from the hospital . . .

Tom Hospital?

Josiah One of our lads got smashed by a jar of pickled onions.

Albert They've just made medical history. The first onionectomy ever performed.

Josiah Aye well, that saves us the cost of a wreath.

Tom But there's been a tarring and triping in Didsbury.

Albert Good God. There hasn't been a tarring and triping since . . .

All Burnley in eighteen ninety-six.

By now, the audience should be joining in, too

Albert But that was in the Burnley Tripe War.

Josiah Aye. I reckon we're on the verge of another Tripe War, lads.

Tom Oh great heavens. Not war. Anything but war. All I hear is talk of war. Everywhere I go. War. War. War.

Tom exits, very dramatically

Act I

Josiah cues and the audience applauds

Josiah What a performer! Give him a big hand!

Applause

But I'm still worried about him.

Albert It's that lad he goes playing darts with on a Friday night . . .

Josiah What's his name?

Albert Bertrand Russell.

Roger pops up again

Roger Shifting sands. Shifting sands.

Roger pops down again

Josiah No question about it, son. It's a full-scale tripe war.

Albert But who's organizing the other side?

Roger I am!

Roger steps on stage and confronts the Fosdykes

Josiah Roger Ditchley!

Albert The swine who besmirched my sister!

Roger And now I'm going to besmirch your Tripe Empire. All the small tripe men in Manchester are behind me. We've taken over Gas Street, Canal Street, Bridge Street . . . (*He sticks flags in the map*)

Albert But we've recaptured Dreg Street and Workhouse Lane with a cut-price red cabbage offer. (*He sticks flags in the map*)

Roger Big deal. We've got gangs of thugs from Salford roaming the streets, intimidating your men.

Josiah Can't we negotiate a tripe-artite settlement, Ditchley?

Roger Make me an offer.

Pause

Josiah I'll bring in gangs of thugs from Oldham.

Roger That's not an offer.

Josiah I know. I've changed my mind.

Roger Right. In that case I'll bring in gangs of thugs from Rochdale.

Albert Good God. Co-operative thugs.

Josiah Thugs from—Birkenhead.

Roger Blackpool.

Josiah New Brighton.

Roger Lytham St Annes . . .

Pause

That's beaten you, Fosdyke.

Josiah No it hasn't. I'll bring in gangs of thugs from—Harrogate!

Roger Yorkshire mercenaries! Right. If it's really a fight to the finish, I'll play my trump card. I'm signing up the O'Malleys.

Roger exits

All The O'Malleys?
Albert Who are the O'Malleys?
Josiah The dirtiest street fighters in the North of England.
Albert Where do they come from?
Josiah Liverpool.
Albert But a gang of thugs from Harrogate can match a gang of thugs from Liverpool, surely ...
Josiah The O'Malleys are women.
Albert Women?
Josiah Yes. They're very tall—they wear green dresses with shamrocks on them. Sometimes they turn up and sometimes they don't.

This is to cover Roger's change into his Emily O'Malley gear. She enters like Marciano

This looks like one now.
Emily Sorry I'm late.
Josiah That's all right.
Emily Mr Fosdyke?
Josiah Aye.
Emily Emily O'Malley.
Josiah Charmed—aagh!

As they shake hands, she fells him

Emily My sisters are strolling along the road from Liverpool. The birds are singing sweetly in the clear blue sky, the flowers are blooming and they're going to smash up a few towns and villages on the way over.
Josiah What is it you want?
Emily My personal friend Roger Ditchley asked me to call in to fix the time of the fight. Outside of your tripe works is favourable with me. Marchioness of Queensbury rules—no kicking above the belt.
Josiah When?
Emily You choose the time.
Josiah Noon tomorrow.
Emily Can you make it one o'clock? I'm at the hairdresser's at twelve.
Josiah One o'clock then.
Emily Shall we shake hands on it?
Josiah Albert. You shake hands on it.

Albert cautiously shakes hands with Emily. She throws him in as spectacular a wrestling or judo throw as can be managed

Noon tomorrow then, Mr O'Malley.

Emily grabs him and knocks a few teeth out

Emily I said one o'clock. And it's Miss.

Emily gives Josiah a full-blooded and fairly nasty kiss, then exits

Albert Why did you agree to the battle, Father?
Josiah (*spitting teeth*) Because nobody calls the Fosdykes cowards. We

Act I

stand our ground and we fight. And we've got till one o'clock tomorrow to plan our tic-tacs—I mean tactics.
Albert Good. Let's plan our tactics.
Josiah I've already planned them. We'll run away. We'll emigrate to America. I'll book tickets on the *Titanic*.

Vicky enters carrying a Suffragette banner

Vicky You won't run away. *We* will fight the O'Malleys.
Albert You? And whose army?
Vicky The Womens' Suffrage Movement Heavyweight Division. Sylvia Pankhurst's out for a month with a groin strain but otherwise we're at full strength.

The M.C. enters—talking and acting like a boxing M.C. and clanking a gong

The screen shows a picture of the exterior of Fosdyke's Tripe Factory

M.C. And there's a record crowd here outside the Fosdyke Factory for the Fight of the Century. You've heard of the Thriller in Manila. Well this is the Slaughtering'em in Altrincham. Fifteen rounds, three minutes each round, to be decided by the best of three falls or a submission—between, in the blue corner, representing the O'Malley sisters and Ditchley's Tripe and Pickle Company—Emily O'Malley!

Emily enters

The audience is encouraged to boo. A few bars of "2001 Space Odyssey" music are heard as the M.C. introduces Vicky

And in the red corner, representing the Womens' Suffrage Movement and Fosdyke's Tripe ... Victoria Fosdyke!

The audience is encouraged to cheer. Vicky is manoeuvred into position. Her arms are chained to a length of iron railing on a stone base

Josiah She can't fight chained to a length of iron railings.
Vicky Have faith, Father.
Josiah But if I'd known you were going to be in chains, I'd have got better odds than five-to-two.

The fight proceeds. The general pattern is that Emily attacks and demolishes everybody in sight, not excluding members of the audience. The audience is encouraged to boo Emily and cheer the motionless Vicky. Emily disregards Vicky, since she is chained to the railings anyway. Eventually Vicky sneaks up behind Emily and swings her arms, chains, railings, stone plinth and all, and CLUNKS Emily to the ground. Cheers and reactions follow, verging on mass hysteria. Tom leaps up on a soapbox in front of the factory

Tom Stop, all of you! Have you all gone mad? Has the world gone mad?
Josiah *He's* gone mad.
Tom On this lovely Tuesday or Wednesday in nineteen thirteen, or fourteen, why are we all fighting each other? O'Malleys fighting Suffragettes?

Fosdykes fighting Ditchleys? While across the broad acres of Europe, the nations are girding their loins for battle. (*He continues speaking through the following exchange*)

Josiah Do you think young Tom's going all pacifist?
Albert I reckon he must be—once you start talking about girding loins, you're generally in trouble.
Josiah I never thought I'd live to see a son of mine refuse the call of King and Country.
Becky You're just a bullet-headed bigot, Josiah Fosdyke. There's thousands of folks in this land feel exactly the same way as our Tom.

Josiah exits

Tom My friends. Let us find peace in our time. Nation shall speak peace unto Nation. Great Britain shall speak peace unto Germany. France shall speak peace unto Italy. Japan shall speak peace unto Russia.
Emily Just as long as the Irish can go on fighting among themselves, that's all right.
Tom My friends . . .

Josiah returns with a large sack containing white feathers

Albert Where have you been, Dad?
Josiah Patterson's Pillows and Palliasses. I've bought up all the white feathers in Manchester. Support our local boys in France—send a feather to a nance. I'll make a bloody fortune.

Josiah gives feathers to the audience as Tom continues

Tom Don't listen to the men of violence, listen to the men of peace. Don't listen to the field-marshals and the generals—listen to the poets and the peasants.

As Tom speaks we hear the sound of a Zeppelin

Listen to the sweet and tender sound of peace.
Albert I can't just hear it, I can see it an' all . . .

We see a Zeppelin—in reality a cutout or small inflatable on a wire—hovering above the screen and the factory

Becky It's heading straight for t'Tripeworks!
Josiah Flat on the ground, everybody!

Everybody lies flat on the ground

A German Airman straightens up behind the screen. In his hand is a cut-out bomb marked "BOMB"

Airman I'm sorry. I'm just carrying out orders. (*He drops the bomb*)

Black-out. Explosion. The Lights fade up on rubble and devastation and everybody picking themselves up. Tom is now angry

Act I

Tom Well really! So this is your idea of war, is it? Bombing an unarmed, defenceless Tripe Factory . . .

Josiah No, no, no, it isn't as simple as that, son. Obviously they knew we'd been doing confidential work on secret weapons—bouncing black puddings, detonating cowheels . . .

Tom I don't care. I'm going to fight them. Let us shake hands like men.

They shake hands

Josiah Well done, son, I'm proud of you.

Cheers

This can only mean one thing.

Becky What's what, Jos?

Josiah (*with a nod to the audience*) Swift medley of war songs and race these buggers to the bar.

The War Medley starts up—a marching song, complete with awkward squad drill routine to taste

Chorus We're going to knock the helmet off the Kaiser
We're going to cut the Urals off the Czar
We will march along the Somme
With a tiddly-om-pom-pom
And still be back in time to have a jar.

We're going to rape and pillage with abandon
We're going to act like Saxons, Danes and Celts
We will make Attila the Hun
Seem like lots of jolly fun
With virgin scalps a-dangling from our belts.

We're going to loot and plunder with discretion
And if we're smart we'll lord it through the war
When the shells begin to fly
It won't be us that die
Cos we'll be in the Army Catering Corps
Cor blimey
We'll be in the Army Catering Corps.

Vicky and Becky sing their tender ballad, taking alternate lines, and singling out a series of innocent male citizens in the audience for their attentions—sitting on knees, gently kissing, both fancying the same bloke, etc.

Vicky ⎱ Oh Johnny I don't want to lose you
Becky ⎰ Dear Harry I want you to stay
Sweet William I'd love to amuse you
But Richard you must go away.

Oh David I'll miss you so badly
Dear Albert my heart beats so fast
Sweet Henry I love you so madly
But Ernest it simply can't last.

> Oh Charlie I'd love to repeat it
> Dear Fred with emotion I gulp
> But my husband says if you don't beat it
> He'll smash you all into a pulp.

Now they all go into the final big one which is a poor, underprivileged cousin of "Land of Hope and Glory".

Chorus   The Red, White and Blue
          Protects me and you
          Trusted and true
          In everything we do
          You'll see what we do
          To foreigners who
          Think they can screw
          The Red, White and Blue.

Josiah (*shouting*) Next verse!

This involves a marginal change in tune, but not much. It is all accompanied by much standing to attention, saluting flags, etc.

Chorus   None shall attack
          The Union Jack
          None shall usurp
          The Crown
          We shall defend
          The Empire too
          And every other pub in town.

Josiah All together now! In your programmes! On the song sheet!

The audience joins in from a song sheet in the programme or on the screen

All   None shall attack
       The Union Jack
       None shall usurp
       The Crown
       We shall defend
       The Empire too
       And every other pub in town.

The song comes to a big finish—can be repeated, if desired, at a faster pace, and at the conclusion they all rush off to the bar

ACT II

The House Lights go down. The screen shows the Western Front

Becky walks on, into a spot

Becky Ladies and gentlemen. In the second half of our show you will see the working-class of Europe manipulated by the forces of world capitalism thrust into an ongoing counter-productive war situation. The time is the winter of nineteen fourteen or fifteen. The place: the Western Front.

Tom plays mouth-organ, while Albert, in Royal Flying Corps uniform, is writing a letter home

Albert Nineteen fourteen, or fifteen. The Western Front. "Dear Mum and Dad. At last I'm in France, ready to have a crack at the Boche. It's great fun in the Royal Flying Corps and my instructor says I handle my controls like a veteran. Today I met my new commanding officer." (*He straightens up to attention and salutes*) Lieutenant Fosdyke reporting for duty, sir. New replacement from Blighty, sir.

Roger enters in uniform

Roger Squadron-Leader Ditchley. (*He salutes, oddly*)
Albert (*semi-aside*) Good grief! It's Roger Ditchley, the man who ravished my sister!
Roger (*semi-aside*) Fosdyke! Not that strumpet's young brother?
Albert You filthy swine! (*He seizes him by the throat*)
Roger Sir!
Albert You filthy swine, sir.

The sound of aeroplanes is heard. Albert puts Ditchley down

I'm sorry, sir. Our personal differences must wait until the war is over.
Roger That's a good, patriotic attitude, Fosdyke. It isn't *my* attitude but it's good and patriotic.
Albert Listen!

The aeroplanes are getting louder

Is that the enemy, sir?
Roger It could be Amy Johnson in Concorde for all I know. Let's have a look. (*He trains binoculars on the audience. To a selected girl in the audience*) Be careful how you're sitting, darling. Yes, by God, it's the Boche! Hundreds of the evil Fokkers. The aeroplanes look pretty nasty as well. Tell you what, Fosdyke . . .
Albert Sir.

Roger Seeing as this is your first day in the squadron . . .
Albert Sir.
Roger I'm going to grant you a special dispensation.
Albert Sir.
Roger Someone may well be killed.
Albert Sir.
Roger And quite frankly, Fosdyke . . .
Albert Sir?
Roger We'd like it to be you. I want you to fly my specially equipped aeroplane. Lead my brave boys into battle.

Roger hands Albert the aeroplane—a simple cutout affair with a piece of string running from the wings to Ditchley's hand

Albert Gosh. Thank you, Squadron-Leader—sir. (*He climbs into the aeroplane*)
Roger Meanwhile, I will undertake another particularly dangerous mission.
Albert A dangerous mission?
Roger Yes. Auditing the mess accounts. Good luck, Fosdyke. Off you go. May God fly with you.
Albert Thank you, sir.
Roger That's right, old boy—in you get. Chocks away. Contact!

The engine roars into life—which might be simulated either naturalistically or musically or both: "R.A.F. March Past" or "Dam Busters", say

Away you go, Fosdyke, into the blue horizon, into the great unknown, to glory for Great Britain and the Empire.

Roger waves Albert off. Albert takes off. He hovers against the screen, which shows a picture of the sky speckled with aeroplanes

Now to operate the top-secret equipment.

Fosdyke pulls the string. The aeroplane collapses, into as many fragments as possible. Fosdyke falls

Albert You cad, Ditchley! You've betrayed me! Once a blackguard, always a blackguard!
Roger This boy's no fool.
Albert I suspected as much.

Albert makes a parachute materialize—probably a well-dressed umbrella

Roger Dammit! Can't you die like a man?

Albert lands beside Ditchley

Albert Not while there's a score to settle with you, Ditchley. (*He puts the parachute down, and brings out a wad of papers from inside his jacket*) I was talking to some of the chaps in the squadron while I was up there beyond the blue horizon.
Roger Really? I didn't notice.

Act II

Albert I've taken a few statements. I've got enough evidence to bring you in front of a court martial. Gambling debts. Embezzling the mess funds. Cowardice in the face of the enemy.
Roger Yes, but what am I supposed to have done?
Albert Well, you could be discharged with ignomininy.
Roger You'll have to learn to say it first. Anyway. (*He picks up a piece of aeroplane*) I can pay my debts now. The aeroplane you were flying was insured in my name.
Albert You'll have lost your no-claims bonus.
Roger That's true.
Albert And it still leaves cowardice in the face of the enemy.
Roger Oh, that old thing.
Fosdyke It's a court martial, Ditchley.
Roger I don't believe you.

A Senior Officer enters, in full dress uniform and wallpapered, so to speak, with medals

Officer The Court will rise.
Roger I believe you.
Officer Take the book in your right hand.
Roger I solemnly swear. I also drink, gamble and fornicate.
Officer You are charged with cowardice in the face of the enemy; Fosdyke —the evidence.
Albert Sir. Ditchley was on patrol with young Carruthers . . .
Officer Young Carruthers, eh? (*With a dirty laugh*) You rascal, Ditch.
Albert They were attacked by one enemy machine—it was the Red Baron—Von Richthoven . . .
Officer Von Richthoven, eh? Red Baron, eh? Right. Carry on, Pushbike.
Albert Fosdyke, sir. Whereupon Ditchley waved a white object in the air and flew off leaving young Carruthers to his fate at the hands of Von Richthoven.
Officer Von Richthoven, eh? Young Carruthers, eh? You rascal, Ditchley. A white object, eh? What was this white object, Crossbar?
Albert Fosdyke, sir. Ditchley was seen to jettison the white object over enemy lines—but a suicide squad succeeded in retrieving the said white object with the loss of forty-nine lives.
Officer Forty-nine lives, eh?
Roger Fifty.
Officer Fifty, eh? Call the white object!

This is repeated by everybody on and off stage, ad nauseam

Where is the white object?
Albert In my pocket, sir. I would ask the court to behold—the incriminating white underpants! (*He produces a pair of long white underpants*)
Officer Good God! One gets used to seeing pretty ghastly sights in wartime but . . . Well, Ditchley?
Roger I have a complete answer to all the charges, sir. (*He brings out a wad of papers*)

Officer I should hope so.

Roger Two hundred and thirty-nine signed affidavits from female witnesses in France all testifying that I never wear underpants.

Officer Give me those, Ditchley. (*He hands the Officer the papers*)

Roger What's the matter? Don't you believe me?

Officer I just want the names and addresses, you fool. (*He makes notes*) Jolly good. Now, Ditchley, is there anything you want to say before we have you shot at dawn?

Roger Are you impressed by stories of an unhappy childhood?

Officer Hardly ever.

Roger Very well. It'll have to be—the final solution.

Albert What's that?

Roger I'll sing you a song.

And he does: a vaguely elegant, Jack Buchanan style routine. He has a little help from Albert and the Officer where indicated

> I'm a lily-livered coward and I'm proud of it
> Proud of it
> Proud of it
> I am easily overpowered but unbowed by it
> Unbowed by it
> Unbowed by it.
>
> I can't agree that cowardice is a very ghastly crime
> Especially when I'm paralysed by bullets, shells and slime
> The only bonus being it's a laxative sublime
> And I'm proud of it.

All Yes, he's proud of it.

Roger I'm a shifty slant-eyed waster and don't give a toss
> Don't give a toss
> Don't give a toss
> The military view is I'm a total loss
> A total loss
> A total loss.

Roger I hate the sight of soldiers when they're marching in a line
> I've got a streak of yellow where I ought to have a spine
> I hate the sight of dripping blood, especially when it's mine
> And I'm proud of it.

All Yes, he's proud of it.

Roger I'm a gutless son of Mammon and a filthy swine
> A filthy swine
> A filthy swine
> I am happier with smoked salmon and a jug of wine
> A jug of wine
> A jug of wine.
>
> But no-one should imagine I'm a villain and a crook

Act II

        I should have won a medal and be in the heroes' book
        I saved a hundred thousand lives—I shot the bloody cook
        And I'm proud of it

All Yes, he's proud of it.

Behind the final chorus they tie him up and prepare him for the firing squad

Roger It isn't really funny to prepare to die
        Prepare to die
        Prepare to die
        If they offer the right money I could be a spy
        Be a spy
        Be a spy.

        Now Mata Hari's ventures would be like in primary one
        She couldn't hold a candle to the things I would have done
        I'd even swop my granny for a stick of chewing gum
        And I'm proud of it.

All Yes he's proud of it.

Officer Have you anything else to say, Ditchley, before sentence is carried out?

Roger Yes. Look in my top pocket, Fosdyke.

This assumes that Roger is bound and tethered. Albert looks in Roger's top pocket and brings out a letter

    Read what it says.

Albert It's his medical discharge papers, sir.

Roger You can't shoot a man who's medically unfit.

Officer Let me see that. (*He snatches the letter*) It's true. We can't shoot a man who's medically unfit. We'd be driving a horse and cart through the Geneva Convention. Release the prisoner!

They release the prisoner

    (*to Roger*) Ingrowing toenails, eh?

Roger It's hell inside my boots, sir.

Officer Quick drinkies in the Mess before you run away to Blighty?

Roger Yes! Why not!

They set off for the mess arm-in-arm. As they pass the dumbfounded Albert the Officer turns to him

Officer Fosdyke.

Albert Sir.

Officer See that those underpants are buried with full military honours.

Albert Sir.

Officer (*to Roger*)) Now, what are you having to drink?

Roger I'd love a Babycham.

Roger and the Officer exit

Albert is left holding the underpants. He puts them down and resumes letter-writing

Albert Western Front. Nineteen fifteen, or sixteen. "Dear Mum and Dad."

Tom starts playing the mouth organ

"Since Roger Ditchley departed, things have been very much better. Until yesterday I had shot down forty-three German aeroplanes. Today I was made Squadron-Leader in Ditchley's place. This means I have shot down fifty-six German aeroplanes because Squadron-Leaders get a special exaggeration allowance."

Tom Your turn.
Albert Pardon?
Tom I'm on the Western Front as well and I want to write a letter home.
Albert What are you in?
Tom I'm in the Army. Look. (*He indicates the uniform he is wearing*) Can you play one of these?
Albert I don't know. I've never tried.

Tom hands Albert the mouth organ

Tom I'll make it a short letter.

Albert plays the mouth organ rather badly as Tom writes

Western Front. Nineteen fifteen, or sixteen. "Dear Mum and Dad. Things are pretty quiet here on the Western Front. Just an American called Lewis Milestone looking for locations, the war poet's having a bit of a thrash in No-Man's Land, and some noisy bugger playing a mouth organ."

Albert stops playing

"And then there came the urgent ringing of my field telephone."

A telephone rings, feebly. Tom answers it

Hello, Western Front. Yes Sergeant. What that?... You're outside with ten thousand German prisoners and I have to interrogate them? You'd better send one of them in and keep the others outside.... Yes, this looks like him.

Schmidt enters. Tom surveys him

Now then, Fritz. Let's have your name, number and regiment.

No response

Won't talk, huh? Very well, we have ways of finding things out.

Tom sniffs at Schmidt's uniform

I'd say—Second Battalion—(*He fishes in Schmidt's pocket and brings out a large sausage*)—Fifth Bavarian Deaths Head Infantry Sausage! (*He is triumphant*)

Act II

Schmidt Schweinhund!
Tom Schweinhund? And what's your first name? (*He is intrigued by the smell of the sausage. He is about to take a nibble then hesitates*) It smells good, but—could it be an anti-personnel sausage?
Schmidt Good Cherman sausage, jah.
Tom Come off it—there's no such thing as a good German sausage. (*He has another sniff*) Mind you ... (*He tries a nibble*) Not bad at all, swinehound.
Schmidt Nich swinehound.
Tom Nicholas Swinehound?
Schmidt Schmidt!
Tom Pardon?
Schmidt Schmidt!
Tom First down the corridor, second on the left. (*He eats some more of the sausage*)
Schmidt My name is Schmidt.
Tom Ah, I see. I'm Fosdyke. Tom Fosdyke.
Schmidt Not Fosdyke of Fosdyke's Famous Tripe!
Tom Jah. I mean yes.
Schmidt I am Schmidt of Schmidt's Sauerkraut and Schweinwurst.

They shake hands: instant understanding

Tom Fosdyke and Schmidt.
Schmidt Nein, nein. Schmidt and Fosdyke.
Tom How much is your firm worth?
Schmidt One million marks.
Tom That's about seventeen pounds ten in English money.
Schmidt We could have our head office in Berlin.
Tom Manchester.
Schmidt Compromise.
Tom We'll split the difference. Huddersfield. Just a minute. (*He picks up the field telephone*)
Schmidt What are you doing?
Tom My father says never talk business with ten thousand German prisoners waiting outside. (*On the telephone*) Sergeant! Are the rest of the ten thousand prisoners still there? ... Right. I may be some time. You'd better let them go.

The sound of ten thousand marching feet, accelerating into the distance. Tom brings out a sheet of paper

Now, Schmidt, if you'd like to sign this contract.

Schmidt reads it

Schmidt Oh yes, yes. Oh no, no. This is a bad contract. I cannot sign him.
Tom (*shouting*) Sergeant! I'd like you to negotiate on my behalf.

There is a burst of machine-gun fire. Schmidt dances to avoid the bullets

Schmidt Give me the pen, I'll sign! (*He signs the contract*)

Tom Good lad, Fritz. After the war is over, Fosdyke and Schmidt will bestride the world like a Colossus.
Schmidt There is a piano here. You play him, I can sing.
Tom Yes.
Schmidt Come, let us go.

They go to the piano and do the song. If neither is a piano player, they do the song, C, soft-shoe style, sharing the words as indicated—though that pattern is not compulsory

Tom Nation shall speak tripe unto Nation
Schmidt Und comrades shall speak sauerkraut unto friends
Both There'll be no more war
War is such a bore
We'll eat tripe and vurst till our bellies touch the floor
So ...
Nation shall speak tripe unto Nation
And comrades shall speak sauerkraut unto friends.

The music continues, as Schmidt does the "good German" routine as seen in vintage British war movies

Schmidt We shall be friends, Tom, your country and mine.
Tom No danger. If the money's right.
Schmidt You remember last Christmas? When the firing stopped and we all met in No Man's Land ...
Tom Aye, I remember—we sang carols ...
Schmidt And we exchanged presents—chocolates and cigarettes—showed each other photographs of our families at home—and we played football ...
Tom Aye—thrashed you five-nil—you want to drop that Franz Beckenbauer, he's rubbish ...
Schmidt Look at that, Tom.

They look into the sky

   Becky, as a sexy angel, appears over the screen

Tom Can it be ...?
Schmidt I believe it is ...
Tom The Angel of Mons. Our union is blessed by the Angel of Mons.
Schmidt We cannot fail if we are blessed by a good Cherman Angel.
Tom A good *British* Angel ... (*He waves the contract at Schmidt*)
Schmidt Well—definitely not a *French* Angel.
Tom No chance.

They go back into the song

Tom Nation shall speak cowheel unto Nation
Schmidt Und ve'll sell weinerschnitzel to our friends
Both We will be top dogs
Over Eyeties and the Frogs

Act II

> We will build an Empire in our jackboots and our clogs
> When
> Nation shall sell cowheel unto Nation
> And we sell weinerschnitzel to our friends.

The song comes to a big finish

Tom Where are you going now?
Schmidt I shall crawl away to a barbed-wire compound, there to rot away in misery and confinement for the rest of the war.
Tom Will you post that for me on the way? (*He hands Schmidt a letter*)

Josiah enters with Becky and Vicky. Schmidt hands Josiah the letter as he goes

Tom winds the screen on to a picture of Manchester

Josiah Looks like a letter from our Tom.
Becky Let's see.
Josiah No, lass, I'll read it, it might be important.
Becky I'll read it.
Josiah It might be big words.

Pause. Josiah hands the letter to Vicky

Vicky He says having a lovely time, weather good. He's concluded the negotiations with Schmidt . . .
Josiah Give me that letter!
Vicky And encloses the contracts herein . . .

Josiah snatches the letter and looks at the contract

Josiah Such dedication in the face of duty. This is really grand. Production's up forty per cent and now—a multinational company. We must hide this contract on account of industrial tripeonage. I know—the old Joanna. Even Ditchley wouldn't think of looking in there. Becky. I'm taking you out to celebrate. (*He hides the contract in the piano*)
Becky You mean—a seat in the gallery to see George Robey and his daughter Kitty? A small bag of chips from Ernie's Haddock Parlour?
Josiah Aye, Whichever you prefer, love.

Josiah and Becky exit

Vicky Ah me. There's so little for a girl to do in the evenings, now that all the able-bodied men are fighting in France.

There is a loud knock at the door

> Would that that were an able-bodied man! (*She opens the door*)

Roger Ditchley enters

> Roger Ditchley!

Roger Victoria, my love!
Vicky What do you want, vile monster?

Roger No longer a vile monster, Victoria. A disabled ex-serviceman. I was severely wounded at the front.
Vicky (*sort of checking*) How severely?
Roger Not *that* severely . . . (*He seizes her in his arms*)
Vicky Let me go, Roger. I have a present for you.

He lets her go

Roger A present?
Vicky Wait there.

Vicky goes into the "house" and picks up a birdcage. She returns to Roger and opens the cage

Put your hand out, you naughty boy. Open your eyes. Go get him, Joey—seek, boy, seek!

Roger gives a yell and runs off with the budgie at his throat

There is a sound of galloping hooves, wheels on cobbles: then a crash

Vicky (*to the audience*) He always was shit-scared of budgies.

Becky rushes on

Becky Victoria, there's been a terrible accident. We were waiting at the tram stop and this man ran into the road and was struck a fearful blow—your father's dragging him into the house now . . .

Josiah drags on the unconscious Roger

Josiah Good, God, it's Ditchley!
Vicky What was it that struck him the fearful blow?
Josiah May the Lord forgive me, it was one of our vans.

They peer at the recumbent Roger

Vicky Father—is he . . . ?
Josiah Charlie Bradwell driving. He had no chance. Feller's blind.
Becky But Jos—young Roger—is he . . . ?
Roger (*opening one eye*) One of your vans? I'll settle out of court for a hundred pounds.
Josiah Yes, he's still asking for money.
Roger And the use of the master bedroom while I recover.
Becky There's no harm in him having a nice lie down, I daresay. And a nice drop of my pig's bladder broth'll have him on his back in no time.
Josiah On his feet you mean.
Becky It can work both ways.

Becky goes to the "kitchen". They carry Roger to the "bedroom". They place him on the bed

Vicky It looks as if he's unconscious again.
Josiah Aye. He's not a bad looking lad. He'd make a nice corpse.
Vicky Shh! Let him sleep.

Act II

They all creep away, leaving Roger

Immediately Roger leaps up and looks in the piano

Roger Eureka! I have found it! Or something very much like it. (*Yelling*)

Josiah comes to the room

Josiah Feeling better, are you, lad?
Roger Very much better.
Josiah That's fine. Get out.
Roger I'm not getting out. I've just found some contracts drawn up between Fosdyke's Tripe and Schmidt's Sauerkraut and Schweinwurst—contracts drawn up and signed since the war started. Tut, tut, Sir Josiah—trading with the King's foes . . .
Josiah I can explain everything.
Roger You're a fat, greedy, rapacious, entrepreneur . . .
Josiah Yes, that's the explanation.
Roger Don't worry, Fosdyke, I'll keep my mouth shut.
Josiah Good lad, Ditchley—Roger? May I call you Roger?
Roger For ten thousand pounds.
Josiah Ten thousand pounds!

Vicky and Josiah creep away, leaving Roger

Roger gets up and walks around the estate, so to speak, taking possession. Becky looks on

Roger I shall sleep here in the master bedroom from now on. You've got half-an-hour to clear your rubbish out.
Josiah Could you give me an hour, Roger?
Roger Master Roger to you.
Josiah Master Roger.
Becky Don't let him speak to you like that.
Roger I'll have dinner in bed so nip out and fetch me some champers, smartish.
Becky You're not going to let him order you about, are you?
Josiah Do as he says. Will there be anything else, Master Roger?
Roger I'll take a little rest until dinner arrives.
Becky What's up with you, Jos? Do something positive!

Josiah gives her a straight right to the jaw. She falls in a heap

Roger Yes, that was pretty positive. Good night, all. (*He retires*)

Vicky joins Josiah

Vicky Father! I've never seen you hit Mother before. Not on the chin, anyway.
Josiah It's her own fault. I always trained her to sway back against the ropes.
Vicky Father.
Josiah Yes, Vicky?

Vicky Would you like me to try to get the contracts from Roger using—feminine wiles?
Josiah Feminine wiles? How many have you got?
Vicky I think—enough. (*She does her seductive bit*)
Josiah I knew it would pay off—sending you to that week-end course at Cheltenham Ladies' College.
Vicky I want room to operate.
Josiah Right. I'll shift your mother out the way.

Josiah drags Becky to one side

She's spark out. I might have to chuck a bucket of water over her.

Now we focus on Vicky and Roger. Roger is reclining in the bedroom. Vicky stands C and cues music. What follows is a combined song and strip routine and needs sufficient instrumental bridges in the scoring to cover the stripping mechanics. Obviously we get maximum mileage out of the nature of the clothing—voluminous bloomers, ex-War Department petticoats, et al. The song starts with the softly sung/spoken word "Roger"

Vicky Roger—Roger—Roger . . . (*She sings*)
 Come into the parlour, Roger
 Come into the parlour do,
 Got a little tasty morsel
 I've been saving just for you.

She goes into a stripping routine. Choreographically speaking, she leads him a dance

 Come into the garden, Roger
 Come into the garden, do
 Got a pair of early bloomers
 I would like to pluck with you.

The stripping routine continues

 Come into the kitchen, Roger
 Come into the kitchen, do
 Got a juicy piece of crackling
 I've been warming up for you.

The stripping routine continues

 Come into the bedroom, Roger
 Come into the bedroom, do
 Got a cure for night starvation
 I'm prescribing just for you.

By this time she is down to a large, tent-like nightie

Roger Victoria! Are you trying to tell me something?
Vicky I can't fight your animal attraction any longer, Roger. Do with me as you wish.
Roger Promise me, you haven't brought the budgie with you.

Act II

Vicky He's chained up for the night. Just as I am chained to you, Roger.
Roger Very well. In that case, Victoria . . .

A passionate embrace

License my roving hands, Victoria.
Vicky Do you need a licence?
Roger It's a quotation, you stupid cow! Victoria! (*He fumbles along her leg*)
Vicky What's wrong?
Roger Have you no shame, girl? You should at least conceal your sledgehammer!

He lifts up her nightie to reveal a large sledgehammer tied to her leg. He unties the string, takes the sledgehammer and tosses it away

You little fool! I saw through your feeble plan the minute you came in the room. I have locked the door. Your sledgehammer is indisposed. So you might as well know that the contracts are here. *He opens his shirt and we see the contracts tied with string across his chest)*
Vicky So. You've won. You found the sledgehammer.
Roger Now I shall have my way with you.
Vicky You're forgetting one thing.
Roger What?
Vicky The Accrington brick in my handbag.

Roger reacts, but too late. She crashes her handbag down on his head. Again he falls in a heap. She retrieves the contracts

Father! Mother!

Josiah and Becky join Vicky

The contracts.
Becky Shall I make some more pig's bladder broth?
Josiah No. We'll write to our boys and tell them all is well.

Josiah starts composing a letter

Manchester. Nineteen sixteen, or seventeen.

Tom starts playing his mouth organ

Tom Sorry. (*He stops playing*)
Josiah "Dear Tom. Things are pretty quiet here in Manchester. Young Roger Ditchley got himself knocked unconscious twice and your mother once and it's been a bit foggy."

As they speak the Lights cross-fade from Josiah writing to Tom reading the letter while somebody changes the screen to the Western Front

Tom "Dear Mum, Dad and Vicky. Things are going marvellously here on the Western Front. With Schmidt's help, we have organized a chain of *Cordon Bleu* Prisoner of War camps across Europe. At Stalag Luft twenty-seven, near Obergurgl, we are serving *Tripe à la Napolitan* with Wigan Sauce followed by a dirty continental cabaret . . ."

The Lights focus on Josiah, writing to Albert

Josiah "Dear Albert. Things are pretty quiet here in Manchester. Roger Ditchley burned our house down in revenge for what we did to him in the way of knocking him unconscious but we were well insured and managed to save the budgie. Also your mother. The fog seems to be lifting a bit but not very much."

Albert enters in his aeroplane—again, a two-dimensional cutout, with special qualities that will become apparent

Albert "Dear Mum, Dad and Vicky, also budgie, which I am please to hear is well. I am writing this while waiting for Von Richthoven, the famous Red Baron, and celebrated air ace. I meet him ten o'clock most mornings for a friendly joust."

A loud Wagnerian fanfare sounds

"That sounds like him now. I'm pleased to hear about the fog. Love, Albert." (*He puts the letter in an envelope and throws it over the side of the aeroplane*)

Richthoven enters in his red aeroplane—also two-dimensional

Good morning, Baron.
Baron Good morning, Fosdyke.
Albert Champion now it's bearing up.
Baron The weather is also quite nice.
Albert How's the leg?
Baron Not too bad today. Only seventeen bullets hit me. It is only hurting when I am laughing.
Albert Jolly good. Shall we start?
Baron Ready when you are, baby.
Albert How about chauvinistic jokes to start with?
Baron The Germans have no sense of humour.
Albert You're not a coward, surely?
Baron No, I am not a coward. Go ahead with your jokes, Fosdyke.
Albert Round One. Did you know that Jesus Christ was originally intended to be born in Germany? But they couldn't find three wise men?
Baron I do not understand.
Albert One up to me, Baron, I think.
Baron No, no, no, no. I am knowing a joke, Fosdyke. What is it now? I am remembering a joke. It is coming. *Ja ja*. There was a man who was playing in the orchestra and the orchestra was playing in the Albert Hall and the man is coming late for his performance. He comes sneakingly to his seat and takes his music and then turns to his neighbour and says: "Where are we?" And his neighbour says: "We are in the Albert Hall." (*Which, all being well, dies a death*) Perhaps it is losing something in translation.

Act II   41

Albert Definitely one to me, Baron.

They keep the score with little arrows in their respective planes: though chalk marks or one of the other actors using a scoreboard would be acceptable

Baron Next we will have great composers. Round Two!

He waves a hand and we hear a fragment of Strauss: a Viennese Waltz

Strauss, Johann Sebastian Strauss.
Albert Listen to this, Baron. (*He waves a hand*)

We hear Gilbert and Sullivan: "A wandering Minstrel I"—to which Albert mimes

Baron Confectionery music. A mere *soufflé*. (*He waves a hand*)

Mozart's "Eine Kleine Nachtmusik" is heard

Wolfgang Amadeus Mozart.
Albert Brighouse and Raistrick Brass Band. (*He waves his hand*)

"The Floral Dance" strikes up

Baron Wagner. (*He waves his hand*)

Loud Wagner music is heard

His music is not as bad as it sounds. Follow that, Fosdyke.
Albert Easy. Handel's bloody Messiah. (*He waves his hand*)

A swift "Hallelujah Chorus" is heard

Baron Bloody Handel was bloody German.
Albert Bloody hell.
Baron One to me, Fosdyke.

The score is marked up

Albert Right. How about—impersonations? Round Three.

Albert does his impersonation. Obviously this routine must be adjusted to suit the capabilities of the performer: in the original production these lay in the direction of the great Max Wall

Good evening, ladies and gentlemen, Wall's the name. Max Wall. Standing before you in the flesh. Not a cartoon. You've heard of the Great Wall of China. He was my grandfather. He was a brick. Invited a lady member of the audience out for a meal the other night. Soon as she smiled at me I knew it wasn't going to cost me very much. No teeth. She looked at me with pedestrian eyes. They call them that because they look both ways before crossing. I liked the way her nose swept down— then up—then across. (*Accompanied by the appropriate drum beats, he does the funny walk routine*) Your turn, Baron.

The Baron hesitates then erupts into a Hitler impersonation, complete with screaming hysteria

Baron (*shrieking*) *Es kam ein Mann in die Kneipe, der Blaue Hosentraeger an hatte. Ich habe ihm gesagt, warum traegst du Blaue Hosentraeger? Und er hat gesagt, damit meine Hose nicht zu Boden Fallen.* (*Approximate translation. A man goes into a pub wearing blue braces. He is asked:* "*Why are you wearing blue braces?*" "*He replies: To stop my trousers from falling down*")

Albert is aghast

Albert Who the bloody hell was that?
Baron That was Herr Schickelgruber who has been painting my house.
Albert It's got to be somebody famous—somebody well known.
Baron I know him.

Albert scores the point to himself

All right then, Fosdyke. Now we will have magic tricks. Round Four. Various magic tricks.

To suitable music, first the Baron, then Albert, perform suitable pedestrian magic routines, using tricks purchased from the local jokeshop at minimal cost to the management

Fosdyke. You have no more tricks up your sleeve?
Albert Not one. Same time tomorrow?
Baron Same time tomorrow. Let us zoom off into the heavens together.

Which they do. Albert returns alone, having done one circuit

Albert But there was no same time tomorrow. Some silly bugger shot him down.

Albert climbs out of his plane

That's the trouble with world wars. Somebody always spoils it. (*He sings the song, which should have the feel of a Liverpool-Irish amateur tenor singing just before closing time in a Merseyside pub*)

> Good-bye, Red Baron, good-bye
> There's a big red hole in the sky
> The great hangar in the clouds
> Is running out of shrouds
> Good-bye, Red Baron, good-bye.
>
> Good-bye, Red Baron, good-bye
> There's a big red tear in my eye
> This is not a world that caters
> For Intrepid Aviators
> Good-bye, Red Baron, good-bye.
>
> All the greatest men in flying
> Share this tendency for dying
> Icarus and Leonardo
> Wound up incommunicado
> We keep the left hand in our sight

Act II

But gravity gets us with the right
Richthoven is on the shelf
I don't feel so well myself.

Good-bye, Red Baron, good-bye
You have lost the right of reply
You've wound up life's mortal coil
And you're six feet under soil
Good-bye, Red Baron, good-bye, old friend
Good-bye, Red Baron, good-bye.

For a moment Albert stands C, silent and alone. Then he exits. Becky and Josiah come on. One of them winds the screen on to show MANCHESTER

Becky What did the letter say?
Josiah It said, your son is a war hero and we're sending him home for a rest, yours faithfully, the King. Oh, nice of George, Becky. Nice of George.
Becky Oh yes. Look! There he is!
Josiah That's not the King, that's Albert.
Becky Albert!

Albert enters in civvies and a big droopy raincoat

Becky gives him a hug and a kiss

Albert Why are you kissing me, Madam?
Josiah Albert, it's grand to see you.

Josiah shakes hands with Albert

Albert Why are you shaking my hand, sir? Why are you kissing me, Madam?

Pause

Josiah I'm your father and this is your mother.
Albert I'm sorry. I don't know either of you.
Josiah (*to Becky*) Obviously his experiences at the front have affected his powers of recollection.
Becky I think he's lost his memory.
Albert I wonder, since you've been so kind, could you help me?
Josiah Any way at all, lad.
Albert Who am I?
Josiah You're Albert Fosdyke. My son.
Albert Albert Fosdyke. (*He concentrates*) Is he a decent sort of chap, this Albert Fosdyke?
Becky The finest son a mother could have.
Albert Good. I'd hate not to be a nice person.
Josiah Let's sit him down and we'll try this new-fangled Psychological method.

They help Albert into bed

Becky What method!
Josiah It's psychology. They're all at it in Blackburn apparently. Some feller called Fred invented it.
Albert Fred?
Josiah Aye, Sigmund Fred.
Albert No, I don't think I'm Fred.
Becky What are you doing, Josiah?

Josiah picks up a poker

Don't!
Josiah A sharp crack on the head does nobody any harm.
Becky You could fracture his skull.

Josiah whacks Becky with the poker

Josiah You're right—you should always test these things first.
Becky (*to the audience*) Seven days later.
Josiah How are you feeling, lad?
Albert I feel as if a week has passed by.
Becky He just walks around the streets for hours and hours, day and night . . .

Albert gets up and walks round and round, aimlessly

Josiah Very much like that.

Vicky enters with a newspaper

Vicky Have you seen tonight's edition of the *Salford Trumpet*?
Josiah Bloody rag. Won't have it in the house. Not since they declared my entry invalid in the Spot-the-Ball competition.
Vicky Whatever for?
Josiah I didn't realize they meant the football.
Vicky Never mind that—look at the headline . . .
Becky Let's all look at the headline.

Becky winds the screen on to reveal: SALFORD RIPPER STRIKES AGAIN! A sinister chord is played

Vicky Women found hacked to pieces.
Becky Welter of gore.
Josiah Sounds quite good.

They all look at Albert wandering aimlessly round the stage

Becky Jos—do you think . . . ?
Vicky No—it can't be . . .
Josiah Repeated blows to the head can do funny things to a man, Rebecca.
Vicky Repeated blows to the head?
Josiah I've been trying my psychological poker on him most nights since he got home—mind you, if he's been murdering all these women, I feel a bit responsible. . . .
Gecky Follow him. See what he does.

Act II

Vicky Stop him in the middle of his violent assault.
Josiah But it's coming on to rain.
Becky Take your raincoat. (*She hands him a raincoat*) You'd better take yours as well, petal. (*She gives Albert a raincoat, too*)

Josiah stalks Albert round and round the stage, passing behind the screen. A little night music, sinister to boot, accompanies them. The second time round, drama happens behind the screen—and we might be able to play the silhouette game. We see a Woman. Albert attacks the Woman. Josiah attacks Albert and drags him off. They reappear from behind the screen. Josiah has Albert's coat lifted up over his head, and we cannot see his face

Josiah I'll get you home before anybody recognizes you.

Josiah and Albert return home. Becky and Vicky are waiting expectantly

Josiah It's all right. I stopped him in the very act.
Becky *Which* very act?
Josiah He was about to stab a poor, underprivileged streetwalker.
Becky Well, let's help him off with his coat.

The coat falls from the man's head. The man is not Albert! Instead we see a wild-eyed Salford Ripper

Ripper Aha! Women of the streets!
Josiah Hey-up! That's a bit strong, old lad . . .

The Ripper brings out a gigantic knife

Becky You're definitely not our Albert.

Albert returns from behind the screen, also in a raincoat, somewhat bemused

Albert Why is that man waving a knife at Mrs Fosdyke?
Vicky Careful, Albert—he's got a knife!
Ripper I have no quarrel with men. Only in avenging myself on the opposite sex.
Becky Apprehend him, Josiah. He's mad.
Ripper I must punish interfering, cackling women.
Josiah Pity he's mad, he's got some good ideas.
Vicky Father, stop him!

The Ripper flings himself at Becky, Albert flings himself at the Ripper. Josiah, against his better judgement, gets involved with the both of them. Becky and Vicky stand aside and scream

   There is a blast on a whistle and a Policeman enters

The Policeman flings himself on the heap. A tumbling and rolling routine ensues. Eventually they get up, except for Albert. The whole sequence is played in slow motion to the music from "Shaft"

Policeman J. S. Ripper—I must ask you to come along to the station with me. . .
Ripper I've done nothing. Only rid the world of a few evil, scheming women . . .

Policeman That your bike outside? Brakes are in a shocking state. (*To Josiah*) You all right, sir?

Josiah I think so. He came for me with a knife but—(*he feels his chest*)—something protected me—stopped the knife from entering my anatomy ... (*He brings out a wad of tickets*)

Policeman Twenty-five tickets for the Policeman's Ball. I took the liberty of slipping them in your pocket during the struggle. Very kind of you, sir, that'll be twenty-five guineas.

Josiah I'll put a cheque in the post.

Policeman Thank you, sir. Come on, you ...

The Policeman takes the Ripper off, whistling the "Dixon" or "Z Cars" theme

Albert sits up, rubbing his head

Vicky Are you all right?

Albert I'm Albert Fosdyke. You're my sister Victoria. (*To Becky*) You're my mother ... (*He looks at Josiah*) I know the face, can't just put a name to it.

Becky Albert! You've got your memory back!

Vicky It's good, that psychology, isn't it?

Josiah Keep on belting them, they get better in time.

Albert brings out a copy of the "Salford Trumpet"

Albert Hey—listen to this—in the Stop Press ...

Vicky More well-timed news, is it?

Albert Stockport County have signed a new left-half—the fog's expected to lift in the next three weeks—and the war's over ...

Becky The war's over?

Vicky Yes, look ... (*She winds the screen on to show: PEACE IN OUR TIME*)

Josiah That's a blow. We were doing ever so well. Record profits.

Tom enters

Becky And here's Tom, home from the wars.

Tom With a twenty-year trading agreement all signed and sealed by Herr Schmidt.

Josiah I'll tell you what—this calls for a celebration. I'm going to open that bottle of Newcastle Brown I've been saving since nineteen fourteen, or fifteen. (*Josiah opens a bottle and passes it round*) I'll give you all a toast. The New World.

Albert Yes. The world can never be the same again, after what's happened ...

Becky Well, it's four years later, isn't it?

Vicky I see a brave new land where women can hold their heads high in equality and dignity.

Josiah Albert, fetch me the poker.

Tom No, she's right. I've done some pretty nasty things in the war—we all have—and—quite enjoyed it really ...

Act II

They all go into the song, to a straightforward hymn-type tune

All We will build a New World
We will build it strong
A land of noble visions
A land of wine and song.

Albert We will build homes for heroes
Josiah With gardens for the old } *Singing together*
With streets of beaten silver
And wages paid in gold.

Becky The women will wear dresses
Vicky Of iridescent silk } *Singing together*
A-woven by selected worms
Of Anglo-Saxon ilk

Tom Each evening we'll read poetry
And eat exotic fruits
Each night we'll drink pure nectar
Until we're pissed as newts.

All A land of Hope and Glory
Of little birds that sing
And if you buy this story
You'll buy any bloody thing.
Oh yes we'll build a New World
Oh yes we'll build it strong
They're bringing the components
On a slow boat from Hong Kong.

To the tune of "Amen", they sing

Hong Kong.

Josiah That's the end of a Family at War. The Stars are Looking Down, Our Boat is Coming In. These are Days of Hope, lads. We must expand t'Tripe Empire Albert.

Albert The *Daily Herald* is giving ten thousand pounds for the first man to fly round the world using an aeroplane that doesn't need elastic. I shall be off in the Fosdyke Special tomorrow, with a forty-foot banner publicizing Fosdyke's Worldwide Tripe.

Josiah And what about you, Tom?

Tom I'm going to America.

Becky America? That's yon side of Blackpool, isn't it?

Tom Chicago to be precise.

He waves a quick one-two to the orchestra and sings a short, highly-exaggerated Blues

(*singing*)
>Oh I'm going to Chicago
>To see my baby there
>Oh I'm going to Chicago
>To see my baby there
>She's a proper little cracker
>I know 'cos I've been there . . .
>Oh yeah . . .

(*speaking*) Prohibition. We can make a fortune peddling illicit tripe. I mean, the mob's running it at the moment . . .

Vicky The mob?

Roger pops over the screen, dressed like Capone

Roger The Ditchley mob but he doesn't know that yet. I'll be waiting for you, baby—you dirty rat.

Roger bobs down again

Josiah Well, I'm off to Russia.
Becky Russia? Be careful. What about the Labour Camps?
Josiah That's all right, love. I'll tell 'em I'm a Conservative. Nineteen-seventeen, or eighteen. The proletariat and the bourgeoisie stormed the Winter Palace or the Leningrad Hippodrome—the situation in Russia is something like this . . .

There are a few bars of balalaika introductory music, then Josiah sings
(*Singing*)
>They are boozing on the Battleship *Potemkin*
>They are ringing bells from Volgograd to Rome
>All the Samarkands are brandishing their Tolstoys
>They've always been a banker when at home
>The Mazurkas are revolting on the Volga
>And the samovars are running to the sea
>All the Dostoevskys shout: Tripe for the People
>And I reckon there's a few bob there for me.

A Russian dance follows (*optional*), *and the song ends*

Roger enters; to audience boos, all being well

Roger I've come here to make an announcement, not play silly games with the audience. (*Pause, and change of key*) And so, in all four corners of the earth, the name of Fosdyke became a household word—like Harpic or dustbin. And nations of all colours and all creeds joined together with one voice in singing the famous Fosdyke Anthem. Ladies and gentlemen—please join us in the singing of this uplifting hymn.

Everybody sings

All Fosdykes Arise
Fosdykes Arise

Lift up thine eyes
See the Fosdykes Arise

Tripe it is grand
Tripe it is noble
In every land
Tripe it is global
Better by far
Than fowl, fish or weevil
Let there be tripe
And banish all evil.

Fosdykes Arise
Fosdykes Arise
Lift up thine eyes
See the Fosdykes Arise.

Repeat and repeat until everybody has almost *had enough, then stop*

CURTAIN

FURNITURE AND PROPERTY LIST

NOTE: Most of the props are "lying around" just on or off stage, as indicated in the opening stage direction. In a few cases it might be found more convenient to regard small props as "personal", and these are listed below.

ACT I

On stage: Screen with changeable images
Pit helmet **(Josiah)**
"STRIKE" banner on pole **(Pitman)**
Cloth caps, banners **(Strikers)**
"Baby" with swivel head
Cut-out train carriage
Train whistle
Various musical instruments, as desired
Tray of tripe **(Ditchley)**
Recipe list **(Josiah)**
Sheet **(Vicky, Roger)**
Top hat, trousers, frock coat **(Roger)**
Enrolment form **(Mrs Pankhurst)**
Radical newspaper **(Mrs Pankhurst)**
Document **(Josiah)**
Sparkler or flashbulb **(Reporter)**
Jar of pigs' ears **(Tom)**
Prison officer's hat, bunch of keys **(Reporter)**
Newspaper **(Newsboy)**
Pigeon with message attached
Large jar **(Albert)**
Map flags **(Albert, Roger)**
Suffragette banner **(Vicky)**
Gong **(M.C.)**
Length of iron railing on stone base, chains **(Vicky)**
Soapbox **(Tom)**
Sack of white feathers **(Josiah)**
Cut-out Zeppelin
Bomb **(German Airman)**
Pieces of rubble, etc.

Personal: **Ditchley**: piece of tripe
Becky: diary, pencil
Josiah: piece of black tripe
George V: sword in scabbard

The Fosdyke Saga

ACT II

On stage: Cut-out trick aeroplane **(Roger)**
"Parachute" **(Albert)**
Lengths of rope
Field telephone
Bed and bedding
Sledgehammer **(Vicky)**
Cut-out trick aeroplane **(Albert)**
Cut-out red aeroplane **(Richthoven)**
Small marker arrows **(Albert, Richthoven)**
Assortment of joke shop tricks **(Albert, Richthoven)**
Poker **(Josiah)**
Newspaper—*Salford Trumpet* **(Vicky)**
2 raincoats **(Becky)**
Large knife **(Ripper)**
Newspaper—*Salford Trumpet* **(Albert)**
Bottle of Newcastle Brown **(Josiah)**

Personal: **Tom:** mouth organ, contract, pen, letter, notepaper
Roger: binoculars, papers, letter, contracts tied to chest
Albert: papers, long white underpants, notepaper, pen, envelope
Senior Officer: pen, notepad
Schmidt: sausage
Vicky: handbag with "brick" inside
Josiah: notepaper, pen, wad of tickets
Policeman: whistle
Ripper: raincoat

INCIDENTAL MUSIC PLOT

ACT I

Cue 1	As action starts *Ominous drum roll or fanfare*	(Page 1)
Cue 2	**Josiah**: "I mean Manchester." *Fanfare*	(Page 4)
Cue 3	**Vicky** and **Josiah** get on treadmill *"The Volga Boatman"*	(Page 15)
Cue 4	The **King** enters *Elgar music—repeat on his exit*	(Page 16)
Cue 5	M.C. introduces **Vicky** *Music from "2001—a Space Odyssey"*	(Page 23)

ACT II

Cue 6	**Roger**: "Contact!" *R.A.F. music*	(Page 28)
Cue 7	**Albert**: ". . . for a friendly joust." *Loud Wagnerian fanfare*	(Page 40)
Cue 8	As **Richthoven** and **Albert** alternatively wave hands in their aeroplanes *Fragments of music are played, in the following order:* *Viennese Waltz* *"A Wandering Minstrel I"* *Mozart's "Eine Kleine Nachtmusik"* *"The Floral Dance"* *Loud Wagnerian music* *Handel's "Hallelujah Chorus"*	(Page 41)
Cue 9	To accompany **Albert**'s "funny walk" *Drum beats*	(Page 41)
Cue 10	**Richthoven** and **Albert** perform magic tricks *Suitable accompanying music ad lib.*	(Page 42)
Cue 11	**Ripper** headline appears on screen *Sinister chord*	(Page 44)
Cue 12	**Josiah** and **Albert** enact "Ripper" routine *Sinister night music*	(Page 45)
Cue 13	During fight sequence with **Policeman** *Music from "Shaft"*	(Page 45)

LIGHTING PLOT

NOTE: Essential cues are given below: these may be augmented as facilities permit

Property fittings required: nil

ACT I

To open: Full overall lighting

Cue 1	**Tom:** "There's blood inside." *Black-out. After explosion return to previous lighting*	(Page 3)
Cue 2	**Mrs Pankhurst:** "One, two, three—jump!" *Black-out. After splashing sounds, fade up to previous lighting*	(Page 13)
Cue 3	**Airman** drops bomb *Black-out. After explosion fade up to previous lighting*	(Page 24)

ACT II

To open: Spot on **Becky**

Cue 4	**Becky:** ". . . the Western Front." *Bring up full overall lighting*	(Page 27)
Cue 5	**Josiah:** ". . . been a bit foggy." *Fade to spot on* **Tom**	(Page 39)
Cue 6	**Tom:** ". . . dirty continental cabaret. . . ." *Cross-fade to spot on* **Josiah**	(Page 40)
Cue 7	**Josiah:** ". . . but not very much." *Cross-fade to spot on* **Albert**	(Page 40)
Cue 8	**Richthoven** enters *Bring up overall lighting*	(Page 40)
Cue 9	**Becky** gives **Albert** raincoat *Fade to sinister lighting, with silhouette effect if possible on screen*	(Page 45)
Cue 10	**Josiah** and **Albert** emerge from screen *Fade up to previous lighting*	(Page 45)

EFFECTS PLOT

ACT I

Cue 1	**Actor 4:** ".... five thousand and six...." *Baby cry*	(Page 2)
Cue 2	**Josiah** hammers on "door" *Sound of banging*	(Page 3)
Cue 3	**Josiah:** "Huddersfield Choral Union?" *Pithead bell rings*	(Page 3)
Cue 4	**Albert:** "... by dinner-time." *Pithead bell rings*	(Page 3)
Cue 5	**Tom:** "There's blood inside." *After Black-out—loud explosion*	(Page 3)
Cue 6	"Train" starts *Clanking train noises and smoke*	(Page 4)
Cue 7	**Mrs Pankhurst:** "One, two, three—jump!" *After Black-out—2 splashes, gurgling noises*	(Page 13)
Cue 8	**Becky:** "The anger of the Nation!" *Loud door hammering*	(Page 16)
Cue 9	**Josiah:** "Don't be afraid, Tom." *Door hammering*	(Page 16)
Cue 10	**Tom:** "... poets and peasants." *Sound of approaching Zeppelin*	(Page 24)
Cue 11	**Airman** drops bomb *After Black-out—explosion*	(Page 24)

ACT II

Cue 12	**Albert:** "You filthy swine, sir." *Sound of approaching aeroplanes*	(Page 27)
Cue 13	**Tom:** "... my field telephone." *Telephone rings feebly*	(Page 32)
Cue 14	**Tom:** "You'd better let them go." *Sound of marching feet—fading away*	(Page 33)

| *Cue* 15 | **Tom:** ". . . on my behalf."
Burst of machine-gun fire | (Page 33) |
| *Cue* 16 | **Roger** exits with budgerigar
Sound of galloping hooves, wheels, then a crash | (Page 36) |

www.ingramcontent.com/pod-product-compliance
Ingram Content Group UK Ltd.
Pitfield, Milton Keynes, MK11 3LW, UK
UKHW021847210426
5322IPUK00022B/525